Cornerstones of Freedom

The Story of
THE
SMITHSONIAN
INSTITUTION

By R. Conrad Stein

Illustrated by Richard Wahl

 CHILDRENS PRESS, CHICAGO

Library of Congress Cataloging in Publication Data

Stein, R. Conrad.
   The story of the Smithsonian Institution.

   (Cornerstones of freedom)
   SUMMARY: Describes the contents of the 13 separate
buildings of the Smithsonian Institution in Washington,
the activities of this institution, and its
mysterious origins.
   1.   Smithsonian Institution—Juvenile literature.
[1.   Smithsonian Institution.]   I.   Wahl, Richard, 1939-
II.   Title.
Q11.S8S89   069'.09753   79-12902
ISBN 0-516-04635-7

1 2 3 4 5 6 7 8 9 10 11 12 R 85 84 83 82 81 80 79

Do you love to watch machinery in a technological museum? Are you fascinated by the sight of dinosaur bones in a natural history museum? Do the works of great artists in an art museum excite you?

If you like any of these things, you will love the Smithsonian Institution in Washington, D.C.

The Smithsonian Institution is not just one building. It includes thirteen separate buildings in Washington alone. There are also Smithsonian offices and agencies all over the world.

We will limit our visit to the buildings clustered about the tree-shaded mall that runs between the Washington Monument and the Capitol.

Most first-time visitors to the Smithsonian Institution go directly to the spectacular National Air and Space Museum. One of the newest buildings, it was completed in time for the American Bicentennial in 1976. President Ford called it, "America's birthday gift to itself." And what a birthday gift! The building is three blocks long. Inside is the entire story of flight from balloons to rocket ships.

Entering from the mall we see the "Milestones of Flight" display. Hanging from the ceiling is the first heavier-than-air machine that ever carried a man in flight. In 1903 at Kitty Hawk, North Carolina, Orville Wright lay on this frail craft and flew about 120 feet during his 12-second flight.

On the floor directly below the Wright Brothers' airplane is the Apollo II spacecraft, *the Columbia*. This craft carried the first men to the moon in 1969. Michael Collins, the director of the Air and Space Museum, piloted the *Columbia* around the moon while Neil Armstrong and Buzz Aldrin explored the moon's surface.

It is fitting that the Wright airplane and the Apollo spacecraft are shown together. Sixty-six years passed between man's first flight and the journey that carried man to the moon. Each craft launched man into a new age.

More milestones of flight are to be seen. There is the silver-colored *Spirit of St. Louis*. In this single engined plane a shy young pilot named Charles Lindbergh took off alone from New York in May of 1927. Some 33 hours later he landed at an airfield near Paris. Lindbergh was the first man ever to fly across the Atlantic Ocean. Overnight he became a national hero.

In the years after Lindbergh's flight the speed and weight of airplanes increased. Only a few dreamers believed that any plane could fly faster than the speed of sound. In 1947 an experimental rocket plane was dropped from the belly of a B-29 bomber. It whizzed to the unbelievable speed of 700 miles an hour. The sound barrier had been broken! This orange and white plane, called *Glamorous Glennis,* now hangs in the National Air and Space Museum.

In the great hallway that runs through the center of the building, we see a long line of people. They are waiting patiently before a plastic table. Imbedded in the plastic like a diamond is a flat rock taken from the surface of the moon. Go ahead, touch it. That's what it's there for. How many people on earth can say they have touched a piece of the moon?

Practically everything in the museum is open. Visitors are expected to touch or do things. Push a button and see how a jet engine works. Push another to answer a question about outer space.

Films are shown, too. One theater has a film called *To Fly*. It is presented on a screen five stories tall. The film is so real that some people claim they feel airsick. Another movie shows American astronauts casually walking on the moon. One of them is singing, "While I was strolling on the moon one day."

In the center of the museum is a complete planetarium, The Albert Einstein Spacearium. Inside the room is full of music. Then the lights flick off. Overhead the stars of the Milky Way on a clear, star-lit night appear. The scene shifts. Now we are looking at the deep blue earth as seen from the moon.

The second floor of the museum is devoted to different aircraft. One room shows the development of helicopters. Another has World War I fighter planes. World War II fighters on display include a Messerschmitt, a Spitfire, a Mustang, and a Zero. From the second floor balcony visitors can look down at the famous fighter of the 1950s, the Sabre Jet.

We came to the National Air and Space Museum because it is so popular. In the first six months after it opened more than five million people visited it. There is much more to see, but we must leave now.

Down the mall is the Hirshhorn Museum and Sculpture Garden. Built in 1974, it is the only circular building on the mall. This large building is raised from the ground and supported by four huge piers looking like feet. Somehow the building gives the viewer a feeling of lightness. It looks as if it could use those feet to dance right out of its foundation.

The Hirshhorn Museum houses some 4,000 paintings and 2,000 sculptures. Its wide hallways are bathed in sunlight that streams through the row of windows stretching along the inner open core of the building. The works vary, but the central theme is American Art of the 1900s. Some of the great modern painters are represented, such as Edward Hopper, Jackson Pollock, and Robert Motherwell. There are also paintings by famous artists of the late 1800s, such as Winslow Homer and Mary Cassatt.

Outside the circular museum is a lovely sculpture garden. The garden is a perfect place to rest and gaze at the dozens of sculptures, while planning our next stop.

The Arts and Industries Museum might be considered America's one hundredth birthday present to itself. It was built to store items displayed during the United States' Centennial celebrated in Philadelphia.

The United States was a supremely confident nation in 1876. That confidence was based on technology. Railroad tracks were crisscrossing the country. Factory buildings were rising. Cities growing. People believed that industry was the answer to all problems, and that machines could do everything. This faith in technology can be seen in the vast number of fascinating machines in the museum.

There is a steam locomotive that once was used to race passengers and freight from city to city. It is in such good shape that it looks like it could still pull a dozen cars.

Electric motors had not been developed by 1876, so all around us we see steam-powered pumps, printing presses, and machine tools. There is also a 42-foot-long model of a steam-powered warship, the *Antietam*, once the pride of the navy.

In a glass case are miniature machines whose inventors once applied for patents at the U.S. Patent Office. Some of these machines were successful, such as the sewing machine designed by Mr. Singer. Others were less successful—"a device for loosing boots and shoes," a "machine for butting up bottom pants," a "tool for splitting whale bone."

The Smithsonian Institution has been called our "national attic." A place where we store things that are old, but still dear to us. Strolling through the Arts and Industries Museum and seeing the outdated but still fascinating machinery, we know how the Smithsonian earned that name.

Our next stop is the original Smithsonian building. Because of its appearance it is known as "the castle on the mall." Completed in 1855, the building was

designed by the same architect who designed St. Patrick's Cathedral in New York City. Today the castle is used mainly for offices. But it stands as a reminder of the Smithsonian's unusual history.

The Smithsonian Institution exists because of money from one of the most mysterious wills ever written. James Smithson was a bachelor whose only love was science. He was born into a very wealthy English family. He went to Oxford University where his favorite subject was chemistry.

Upon the death of the other members of his family, James Smithson became the sole owner of a huge family fortune. In his will he left his fortune to his nephew. But Smithson added that if his nephew should die without children the money should go to the United States, "to found in Washington, under the name Smithsonian Institution, an establishment for the increase and diffusion of knowledge among men." His nephew died, childless. Smithson's rich estate now belonged to the United States.

James Smithson had never visited the United States. To this day no one really knows why this lonely Englishman left his fortune to a country he had never seen.

In 1838 one hundred and five bags containing about 100,000 gold coins were shipped to the United States. The value of the gold was estimated at a half a million dollars. At that time those one hundred and five bags held perhaps the richest single fortune in the world.

A lively debate broke out in Congress. Some congressmen even wanted to send the money back to

England. Senator John C. Calhoun said, "It is beneath our dignity to receive presents from anyone." But former President John Quincy Adams wanted to see the will carried out exactly as James Smithson requested. Adam's idea won. A law establishing the Smithsonian Institution was passed by Congress in 1846.

The Freer Gallery of Art stands near the castle. This magnificent collection of Oriental art also came to the Smithsonian as the result of a will. In 1906 Charles Lang Freer, a Detroit industrialist, left his collection to the nation. President Theodore Roosevelt called the gift "one of the most valuable collections which any private individual has ever given to any people."

The Freer Gallery houses more than 12,000 items. The oldest exhibit is a collection of Chinese bronzes some of which date back to the 12th century B.C. Serious students of Far Eastern art flock to the Freer from all over the world.

We leave the Freer Gallery and cross the mall to the buildings on Constitution Avenue. Before the

opening of the Air and Space Museum, the most
popular Smithsonian building was the Museum of
History and Technology. Perhaps this is the hap-
piest building of all. It is dedicated to the genius of
the American people—their inventions, technology,
and craftsmanship. Here we can see Samuel Morse's
telegraph, Eli Whitney's cotton gin, Alexander
Graham Bell's telephone, and a printing press used
by Benjamin Franklin. The History and Technology
Museum opened in 1964, and its collections total
more than 17 million objects.

Entering from the mall side we see the original
Star-Spangled Banner. This is the same flag that
Francis Scott Key saw over Fort McHenry in 1814.
The sight of that flag still flying after a furious bat-

tle with the British fleet inspired Key to write the words of what is now the national anthem of the United States.

Many visitors are drawn to the exhibit of American farm machinery. Here we can compare wooden plows used during colonial times with plowing devices still in use today. There is a huge, clumsy-looking steam tractor built by the Huber Company in 1921. In the center of the display is a huge combine, harvester-thresher, made in 1886. This monster had to be pulled by a team of twenty horses.

Another popular exhibit is the live beehive. As many as 60,000 bees buzz about in a glass hive. The bees leave the museum through a glass tunnel to feed on the many flowers growing in the mall. They return again to the hive just like their wild cousins.

Transportation is a major theme of the History and Technology building. On the first floor is a covered wagon, just like the ones that carried hundreds of families West. There is also a Haynes Automobile built in 1894. Near it is a 1903 Oldsmobile, and a 1913 Ford, Model-T. Leaning on a kick stand is a 1913 Harley Davidson motorcycle.

At one end of the building we hear the deep whistle of a steam locomotive. Parked side by side are representatives of the early days of railroading and its golden age of the 1920s. There is a 1851 pot-bellied engine with an elongated smoke stack. It weighs 12½ tons and once hauled cars on the Cumberland Valley Railroad. To the right is a huge, 280-ton passenger engine made in 1926 when railroad travel reached its golden age. Nearby is an electric streetcar that rolled through the streets of Washington, D.C. during the turn of the century.

Go upstairs and step into the past. In the photography exhibit we see photographs taken during the Crimean War and early photography equipment. We can also operate penny arcade "moving picture machines" that were popular during the 1890s. In one we see a slapstick comedy about two men trying to hitch a horse to a wagon.

In the news reporting section we can see an early television set. It is about four feet tall and heavy enough to have to be carried by two men. Yet its picture screen is not much larger than the face of an ordinary flashlight. The television set still works. Today it is showing the crowds in New York's Times Square celebrating the end of World War II.

On the second floor is the First Ladies' room. Displayed here are the gowns worn by women attending the inaugural balls given to honor the new Presidents of the United States. The gown worn by Martha Washington is here. So is the gown worn by the very fashionable Jacqueline Kennedy. The exhibit presents two centuries of fashion in America.

You can spend days in the History and Technology Museum, but it is time for us to move on.

The Museum of Natural History is one of the world's great centers for the study of man and his planet. Some of its fossils are three billion years old. It has marvelous skeletons of huge creatures that once walked the earth. We see only a tiny portion of the objects owned by the museum. Other specimens are not on display. They are being examined by scientists engaged in research. The original Natural History building was opened in 1911. The east and west wings were added in the 1960s, doubling the floor space.

Upon entering the museum from the mall side, visitors are greeted by a huge stuffed elephant standing in the rotunda. This African bush elephant is the largest of its species ever found. He stands more than thirteen feet tall and weighs eight tons.

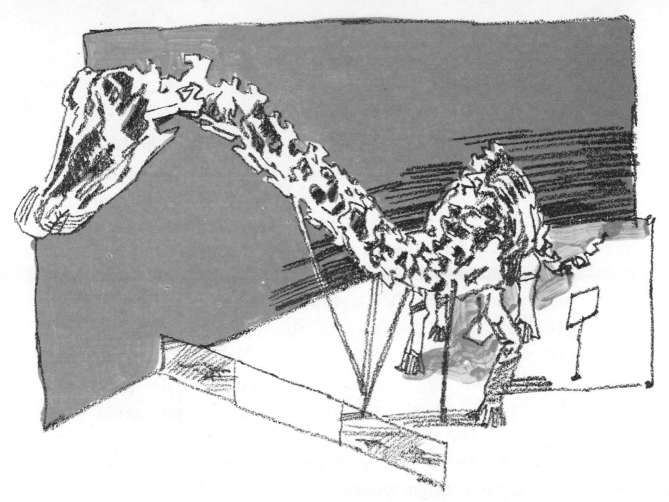

A highlight of the Natural History Museum is the sprawling display of dinosaur skeletons. An eighty-foot-long Diplodocus stands in the center of the room. This giant died stranded in a mud pit in the state of Utah 135,000,000 years ago. The mud hardened into stone, and it took three men seven years to chip the rock off the bones to present a clean skeleton. We also see a delicate five-foot-long Camptosaurus and an armour-plated Stegosaurus.

Walking through the first floor is a walk through geological history. Leaving the age of the dinosaurs we enter the age of mammals. Wall paintings reveal plant life with rodent-like early mammals scampering about. Next we enter the ice age and see a reconstruction of a giant woolly mammoth. In a display case is a 25,000-year-old mammoth tusk. It had been beautifully decorated with a chisel or a knife by some Stone Age artist.

The Discovery Room at the Natural History Museum is great fun. This room is set aside especially for children who want to hold in their hands mammoth teeth, elephant tusks, and fossils more than a billion years old.

Upstairs is the gem room where display cases hold brilliant crystals and large pearls. There is even some of the original gold discovered at Sutter's Mill. This discovery started the California gold rush of 1849.

The most fabulous gem in the world, the gleaming Hope Diamond, is here. Because of its color it has been called the "blue mystery." The Hope Diamond is said to bring tragedy to its owners. One of the owners lost her nine-year-old son in a car accident. Later her husband went insane. Then her daughter died of an overdose of sleeping pills.

Will the Hope Diamond bring bad luck to the Smithsonian? Not likely. It was donated to the Museum of Natural History by a New York jeweler in 1958, and there has been no sign of bad luck yet.

The next building on the mall is the National Gallery of Art. The Statue of Mercury stands in the rotunda. With wings on his feet, Mercury was the messenger of the gods of ancient Greece. This bronze statue was completed in 1613 probably by the Dutch artist Adriaen de Vries.

One gallery is devoted to Renaissance art, a time when artists broke away from religious painting and began to explore the world around them. We stop at the portrait of a young lady painted by Leonardo da Vinci. It is an early work of the master, but we know by looking at it why Leonardo was one of the leaders of the Renaissance.

We come to the *Self-Portrait* painted by Rembrandt in 1659. Unlike many other painters,

Rembrandt was successful and wealthy as a young man. But in later life he faced bankruptcy and many personal problems. This self-portrait was painted when the artist was fifty-three. Do we see a hint of bitterness in the artist's eyes?

In the gallery of American art there is a famous painting done by John Singleton Copley in 1778. The painting was commissioned by a wealthy British merchant, Brook Watson. He had once worked as a sailor. While swimming in the waters off Havana, Cuba, Watson was attacked by a shark. He survived the attack and later asked Copley to retell the event in a picture. Copley captures the horror of the attack so well that we can share the terror of the young swimmer.

One of the liveliest periods in all art history was that of the French Impressionists. These artists were competing with photographers around the turn of the century. To do so they opened up their paintings with their own ideas of light, color, and movement. The room itself seems to brighten when we examine the Impressionist masters—Claude Monet, Auguste Renoir, and Edgar Degas.

The National Gallery of Art often has exhibits on loan from foreign countries. In the early 1960s Leonardo da Vinci's masterpiece, the *Mona Lisa*, was shown. In exchange for this picture, the Smithsonian sent the Hope Diamond to the Louvre in Paris for a special showing. In 1976 the wonders of ancient Egypt came to the National Gallery. The treasures unearthed from the tomb of King Tutankhamen were on display.

In the summer of 1978 the National Gallery of Art opened its new East Building. On display in this marble structure are more than 1,000 paintings, 16,000 rare books, and 90,000 photographs. All of them donated by businessmen.

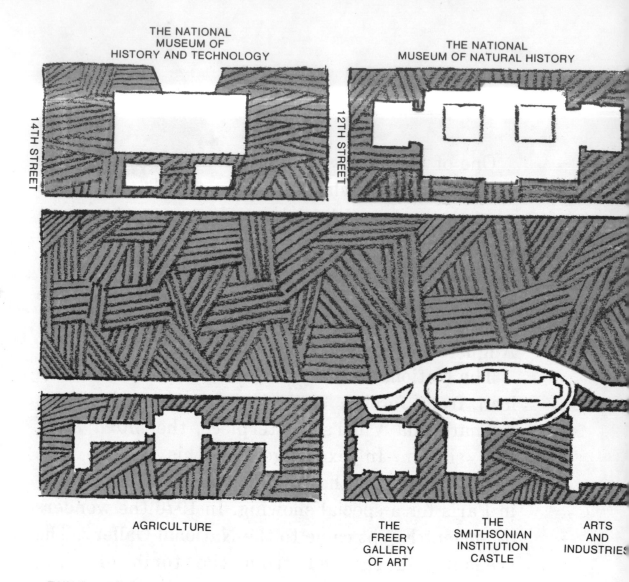

THE NATIONAL
MUSEUM OF
HISTORY AND TECHNOLOGY

THE NATIONAL
MUSEUM OF NATURAL HISTORY

14TH STREET

12TH STREET

AGRICULTURE

THE
FREER
GALLERY
OF ART

THE
SMITHSONIAN
INSTITUTION
CASTLE

ARTS
AND
INDUSTRIES

BUILDINGS ON THE MALL

Well, that's the end of our visit to the buildings on the mall. But there are other Smithsonian buildings to see in Washington. The National Collection of Fine Arts, the National Portrait Gallery, and the Renwick

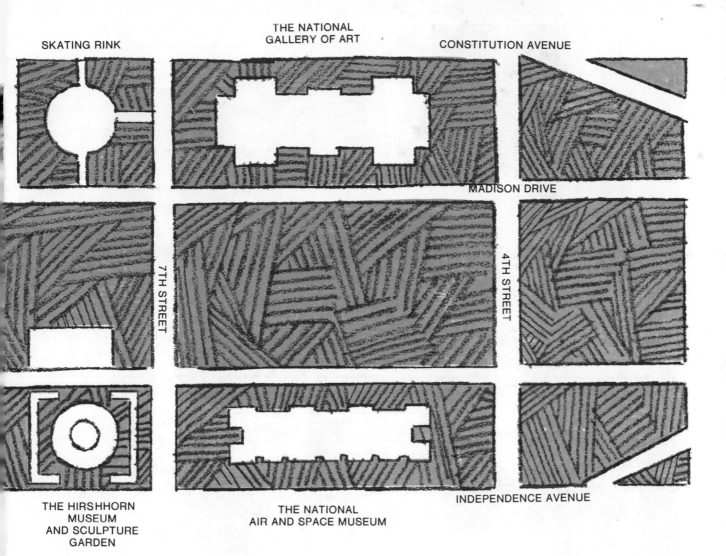

SKATING RINK

THE NATIONAL
GALLERY OF ART

CONSTITUTION AVENUE

MADISON DRIVE

7TH STREET

4TH STREET

THE HIRSHHORN
MUSEUM
AND SCULPTURE
GARDEN

THE NATIONAL
AIR AND SPACE MUSEUM

INDEPENDENCE AVENUE

Gallery all display items that reflect America's cultural heritage. The National Zoological Park and The Kennedy Center for the Performing Arts are also vital parts of the Smithsonian complex.

29

Yet there is more to the Smithsonian. James Smithson's will established an institution "for the increase and diffusion of knowledge." This means more than buildings. The Smithsonian sponsors archaelogical "digs" in all parts of the world. It operates astrophysical observatories and research laboratores. It publishes a monthly magazine. It is the official American agency for the international exchange of scientific and scholarly publications. It collects and distributes information in the life sciences, physical sciences, and social sciences. It grants scholarships. It is involved in almost every aspect of America's scientific and cultural life.

James Smithson probably never dreamed his institution would become so successful. But it did, and Americans owe an enormous debt to this unusual English scholar.

ABOUT THE AUTHOR:

Mr. Stein was born and grew up in Chicago. He attended the University of Illinois and graduated with a degree in history in 1964. He now lives in the Mexican village of San Miguel de Allende where he writes books for young people.

To write this book Mr. Stein went to Washington, and joined the thousands of tourists visiting the Smithsonian Institution. Mr. Stein has been a "museum freak" all his life, and was enchanted by the marvelous displays he saw there. The employees of the Smithsonian Institution helped him tremendously. He wishes especially to thank Mrs. Whitehorn, a volunteer worker at the Smithsonian.

ABOUT THE ARTIST

Richard Wahl, graduate of the Art Center College of Design in Los Angeles, has illustrated a number of magazine articles and booklets. He is a skilled artist and photographer who advocates realistic interpretations of his subjects. He lives with his wife and sons in Libertyville, Illinois.